Cyclorama

POETS OUT LOUD

Elisabeth Frost, *series editor*

Cyclorama

Daneen Wardrop

Fordham University Press   New York   2015

Fordham University Press has no responsibility for
the persistence or accuracy of URLs for external
or third-party Internet websites referred to in this
publication and does not guarantee that any content
on such websites is, or will remain, accurate or
appropriate.

Fordham University Press also publishes its books
in a variety of electronic formats. Some content that
appears in print may not be available in electronic
books.

Visit us online at www.fordhampress.com.

Library of Congress Control Number: 2014952817

Library of Congress Cataloging-in-Publication Data
is available from the publisher.

Printed in the United States of America

17 16 15 5 4 3 2 1

This work was supported in part by an award from
the National Endowment for the Arts.

This work was also supported in part by a grant
from the Faculty Research and Creative Activities
Award, Western Michigan University.

Contents

Daneen Wardrop's *Cyclorama* *Kimiko Hahn*

"It's hard to tell what a thing is."

If a dramatic monologue is an inadvertent self-portrait, it is of course an ironic one since the figure's voice issues from the writer. That self-portrait is complicated further by the writer's own attributes. Of course Daneen Wardrop is not Sophronia Bucklin, an underage Civil War nurse; she is not Sarah Emma Edmonds, a woman disguised as a male field nurse or an Irish peddler woman or a black slave; she is not Lowell, a soldier who tries to itch one phantom limb with his other phantom limb. But, when the writing is really good, as in *Cyclorama,* the poems reveal a self-portrait of the writer herself.

In *Cyclorama,* Wardrop gives us a collection of persona poems, voices from the American Civil War. Such an idea-driven project is not unusual. In successful books, though, the writer touches nerves and deepens themes that belong to herself and to the array of characters. Let's call them conjoined themes: seeing what someone looks at/*observation*, telling what something is/*identification* and *naming*, departure/*loss*, departure/*relove*, disguise/self, . . . and disguise/*trick*.

The cyclorama is a technological "trick," a series of panels that surround a viewer 360° so he or she can experience an event or scene. Think of it as an early virtual reality. Disguises are tricks as well, especially in eluding danger, as Sarah Emma Edmonds does when she crisscrosses Union and Confederate lines. By opening the collection with the poem "Sarah Emma Edmonds," its repeating phrase "See me now" becomes a useful guide for reading the other poems. With these words, Wardrop sets up this persona, the dramatic monologue as a dominant form, and, more important, she presents the trick of disguise as a thematic arc. "See *her* now," both speaker and poet.

When Wardrop touches her own psychological nerve—as with that insistent "See me now"—she touches the reader's nerve. Now see the finely developed craft: the cadence of *storm-clenched days*, the diction of tumult and solitude, and a lyricism that holds all. Threaded throughout are italicized lines and phrases from original sources that I imagine come, at least in part, from her academic research. For "Cornelia Hancock," Wardrop quotes from her letters: *It took nearly five days for some three hundred surgeons to perform the amputations.* And, *Ham, Eggs, Oyster pie,*

Roast Beef and potatoes, peach tarts and cup custards. And *I am safer here than in the attic at home.*

Susie King Taylor says, "It's hard to tell what a thing is." It is hard for them and for us it is hard, too, because we can't always recognize or know what a thing actually is, especially if the trick of disguise or technology is in play. And of course, it is hard to tell what a thing is because the telling can be fraught with intense emotions. Daneen Wardrop places the reader square in the center of her panoramic panels and bids us experience the scenes 360°. What a glorious way to enter these histories. With her, discover how deep empathy can travel and abide, because *it is* "hard to tell what a thing is."

Acknowledgments

I am grateful to the editors of magazines in which some of these poems appeared:

The Antioch Review: "The War Spirit at Home," "Phantom Limb"
Colorado Review: "Woman at the Fence"
The Iowa Review: "Unnamed Panels: Iridescent panel with green crenellations"
The Madison Review: "The Enslaved Mother, Her Baby, and John Brown," "Process of Drafting in New York"
The Marlboro Review: "Army of the Cumberland Panorama"
Michigan Quarterly Review: "Sarah Emma Edmonds," "Susie King Taylor"
New Letters: "Women's Sanitary Corps"
New Ohio Review: "Union Camp Music"
Notre Dame Review: "Off for the War / Home from the War"
88: A Journal of Contemporary Poetry: "Sophronia Bucklin," "Cornelia Hancock"

Cyclorama

I   WHEN I MUST SPEAK ACROSS

Sarah Emma Edmonds

See me now: I'm a slave boy in the rebel camp. Paint rubs off my hands, and one of the other Negroes says, *"I'll be darned if that feller ain't turnin' white."* I add more silver nitrate.

I write down the position of *fourteen ten-inch mortars, and seven eight-inch siege howitzers*, tuck the paper in the inner sole of my shoe. On picket duty I step into the darkness, and step again one more time, I'm gliding through forest back to the union side.

See me now: I'm an Irish peddler woman, practice a brogue. In between the picket lines I find an abandoned house.

And inside there's red ink that I use to line my eyes, mustard that I make into a plaster for blistering my face, and pepper I sprinkle into a handkerchief. So I can cry on caprice. I pull out earthenware, clothing, quilts, add them to my wares.

In the reb camp I spot a salesman I've seen before, loitering behind the union lines selling newspapers. He's talking about Yankee fortifications, he doesn't notice me.

I'm a nurse—quick, remember—man or woman this time?

I'm a nurse and I hold the one hand a soldier has left. He shifts toward death's all-shifting.

Pull back the tent flap.

Inside, warmth from the bedroll swells toward you, thin smell of bread, sweat. The tent flap in hand, you feel the grain?

Last year in Washington, McClellan and others interviewed me, a Canadian, to determine my patriotism. A phrenology test confirmed large bumps of secretiveness and adventure-love. I was hired.

I write with ink the color of skin.

I write on paper the color of skin, see me now.

Paint rubs off my face—

Back on the union side I spot him again—that newspaper salesman, in our camp, detestable spy. I finger him.

Pass back and forth each side of the line, as a hand in a coat sleeve.

That half-mile between yank and reb lines, I live there, search for left biscuits, butter, tea, and once a whole pie still warm. I eat with one leg crossed over the other.

See me now, but really you don't. You put on your coat and each time I've served dinner to reb officers, sweating under black makeup. Straighten the seam at your elbow.

Who was it held a thumb to stop a spurting artery for three hours while the soldier put his affairs in order, finally had to undo the thumb, and he died in three minutes?

If the cuff chafes your wrist I've found a soldier leaning against a tree, clear-eyed, ready to die, who recognized me and I her, for women, and she asked me to bury her and keep her cover, and I did.

See me now. The wig tilts. The voice cracks. I don't doubt doubt, I ride across the line of it.

I don't seem to be what I am, and the seeming is your weight.

Susie King Taylor

Two or three times a week I walk the path to Fort Wagner overlooking Charleston where outside the fort, skulls lie on the ground.

I toe them out of the path. Sharp with reflected white, eyeholes deep as falling.
Tooth-smooth, they scrutinize.

Which side were they on?—some say enemy skulls, some say the skulls of our boys.

It's hard to tell what a thing is.
Magnolia blooms' distressed hands.

The government hasn't paid our black soldiers yet, of course they will never pay us black women.

I carry carved water in a wooden bucket. Sun thin today, like the paper we wrapped our secret books with before walking downtown Savannah to reading lessons in the L kitchen.

First mission—our boys leave for Edisto and the camp turns lonesome, we know some of them won't come back.

Mary Shaw and I sleep together and get nearly eaten alive by fleas. It seems, *now that the men are gone, that every flea in camp has located my tent.*

The wounded begin to arrive, my husband Sergeant King hurt, some hurt worse. Colonel Higginson wounded, too. *They had to wade through creeks and marshes.* They return *with their legs off, arm gone, foot off,* these men.

Swamp for a kitchen, and all I have are turtle eggs and a few cans of condensed milk. I make a turtle custard. The men enjoy it.

I salve Sergeant King's leg and hip. A reb jumped him, Sergeant King held on. His hip is crushed, but he says the enemy got it worse.

And the government still hasn't paid—now Washington offers the black soldier ½ pay and the men say no, they'll wait for full.

There is no ½ musket, no ½ marching.

As the wounded recover, some doze with exhaustion, like my 120-year-old great-great-grandmother we would set in the sun mornings to get her moving.

Of course Mary and I will never get paid, not even half.

Mary and I hang laundry on the line. It shakes off impatience.

These things should be kept in history before the people.

Our troops went inland, found a deserted town, and at its furthest edge were greeted by slaves, who turned out to be not slaves but rebs in blackface. Opened fire. It's hard to tell what a thing is, until it fires.

I climb up to the ramparts outside Fort Wagner and watch shells explode over Charleston—explosions every fifteen minutes. Some skulls that were hidden in the grass light up.

The week continues: Monday, Tuesday, Sheets, Thursday, Mess-pan, Bandage-windings, Sunday.

We hang sheets wet with water that were wet with blood. We will fold them crisp as duty.

Off for the War / Home from the War

I. OFF FOR THE WAR

There's always something headlong about goodbye.
The canteen swings on your belt next to our son's face.
As he hangs on to both of us
you close the embrace,

      then pick up your sword.
            Sun slides off the branch, pulls at each leaf one by one.

On a cliffside tomorrow afternoon the boy and I and others,
will spread red and white checked gingham cloths secured with bowls of potatoes,
jugs of lemonade. We'll look down the hill

over a blue meadow where troops tack, face each other as if by agreement,
square off, two opposing flags flapping with wind,
in the same direction.

We'll talk of Mr. Lincoln and Mr. Davis,
                  think it only polite to believe in campaigns
as we take fried chicken, our son pulling a wing
      to break the connecting flap that held sky in its recess
            when it pecked at meal in the sand.

Night will come in, a dark surf.

I put away toys and books, and I say to our boy,
Please pick up your crumpled jacket from the floor.

He's left Wednesday under it.

Before you went, husband, you said the war will be over by next weekend.

2. HOME FROM THE WAR

This is where we welcome you home again,
                same season, same 1861, same roses in bloom,
             the fighting over
                      fast as wishing.

Inside the picture, though, I know years of seasons
           when hands smoothed napkins,
      children passed around bread, cheese reconnoitered with the rennet.

I've studied the apple and pear for you, the curtain folds.

I have worn my body.

Our child uses my hand to wave at a neighbor.

Nightwind shapes itself to the keyhole, enters.
The faithful whalebone corset still presses skin.
                  Our time is dividual

as yours, forgetting the cut-ching of bullet, grape and canister, the red moue of cannon.

And so, your sword has been erased now in this picture

and so I ask, will an embrace be able to relove its arms—

3. HOME FROM THE WAR: OFFICERS' EDITION

Again we welcome him home, again it's summer
        and roses lean their identical faces and stretched arms,

but now you wear insignia, gleaming, saber and sash included, whiskers full.

Our child's collar is lace.
My calico, silk.

It's new that a horse snorts plumes in the background—

Foot soldiers walk to their hearts.
Officers ride a wave of remembering
        that all blood is knowing.

Those of us left at home will stanch a look
        and a nightmare,

    the reaching sleep that all through the bed he fights
through all the fights.

The War Spirit at Home

"As she balances her suckling infant so she can read The New York Times's report of the 'Great Victory' at Vicksburg . . . a Northern mother's older children erupt into a mock-heroic celebration . . ."

—MARK E. NEELY AND HAROLD HOLZER

I have a headache of your reading, Mama.
       We walk under feet.
       The chair opens its windows.
       Mama's hair, my coat.
Mama, we want the sword.
Baby won't stamp, Ma, there's no horse.
Baby, you know a broom has no nostrils.
       Papa's horse flickered all over its skin with flies.
       Skin of flies.

Newspaper says. Good things?
Papa's coming back!
       Not tonight. All right.
Show our horse to baby?
       Its nostrils breathe too hard.
Here's parcel paper! We wrap ourselves,
       post to Papa. Make hats.
       One for baby, too.
I pull the kitty on a red ribbon.
       I pull the parade on a red ribbon.
Beat the pot, we march.

Process of Drafting in New York

A hand dips in a wheel.
Three o'clock in the afternoon.
Smoke may tear at faces.

I hate three o'clock in the afternoon.
After the slow, slow roll,
a hand steeping in a wheel.

I loll and reel in my shoulders—
and he, and the one next to me—
smoke may tear at our faces.

On the platform, the man pulls
his blindfold tighter. Shirtsleeves rolled,
he clenches names from the wheel.

Whether we fight in streets at home or in fields
beyond, shoulders tighten to others' shoulders,
smoke will tear at our faces.

Some will go down in the detail.
Some will come up on the ghost-tide.
A hand trips a wheel,
smoke tears at our faces.

Colonel Ely S. Parker

In a field photograph, with his staff, General Grant faces Colonel Parker.

My first name "Ely" sounds like "really." Not my given name, which is Ha-sa-no-an-da, or Leading Name. You may not know which name I lead with.

When Grant turns sideways in his seat to look at me, it's hard to imagine the outlines of the picture will ever cut across tree branches and tent flaps.

We're in the outdoors, no frame. But in a week someone will be able to hold us.

No one will be able to hold the war. When they declare it finished, it will still hang from the bushes and rain on the grass.

I can't be an American but I can be a colonel, can't go to college but can be Grant's war secretary.

When I read about the Indian sharpshooters from Company K of the 1st Michigan, I know they study waiting. They take out each reb artilleryman patiently, until the cannons stand one by one, unmanned.

Those Indian sharpshooters join up, afraid the rebs will make slaves of them.

The Secesh may want to capture Indians, but really they want to capture their rifles. Fish and wolverines and moose carved into the rifle stocks.

〰〰〰

I have a third name, Do-ne-ho-ga-wa, for being grand sachem. Means Open Door—like paper juts in the space between letters.

Words start in my gut, I pull them across my lips and not a hitch of Seneca remains.

When I was young *and translated the crooked Indian language into English & the English back to the same*, I started going *crazy, in getting the two languages mixed into my head.*

When I must speak across this.

Now I can write letters all day.
Now I can write words for Appomattox all day.

Just, when you see a cannon ball coming, duck.

~~~~~~~~~~

Indians don't make good soldiers. Until they are *in* it.

In the field I carry ink in a wooden bottle strung to my buttonhole.

Truth be told, the rest of the general's staff can hardly put two letters together.

When I turned grand sachem I was granted a thickness of skin that would *be seven spans*, to guard against criticism. But sometimes I feel my skin the span of one blink.

Grant and I tighten the look till the shutter snaps under the photographer's shroud.

I don't think much about snapping bullets.

The general rides through enemy fire like he feels no concern. I ride that way, too, but I really do feel no concern.

Minnie balls canny as bats climb and titter around our elbows and shoulders.

Or they don't.

~~~~~~~~~~

I'm from the wolf clan, and Grant is something from that pack himself. Sits with the laziness of a predator not on duty at that moment. Turns sideways in his seat. And catches my eye.

Years before the war, I walked past an Illinois barroom fight with a loud, muzzy man holding off all the others, went in and backed him up. The two of us dusted that bunch off pretty good. The loud man: Grant.

Nothing left but to be friends.

Give me a good barroom, a wolf halloo, run me through on a storm-clenched day.

When those Indian sharpshooters see the rebs' gray uniforms sneaking up on them, they look at their own blue coats.

Next chance they get they'll roll in the dirt, cover that blue
with the colors surrounding them.

~~~~~~~~~~

At Appomattox, I meet the courtly Robert E. Lee.

He shakes hands with each of Grant's staff, but speaks straight to me, says I am *the one real American.*

General, I say, *we are all Americans,*

all Senecas, doors, names, all wolves
at a particular wink.

2   MORE TIMES THAN RETURN CAN MUSTER

Women's Sanitary Corps

Sister, I link arms with you
as we enter this log-steepled tent,
white on the outside,
but on the inside the deep maroon
of thick-spackled, internal things.
How can it be
so simple here? Bed,
man—bed, man—
where the pain leaves
no room for anything else.
My mouth is dry.
No, stay with me,
these sheet-smoothed
boys need us
with their nocturnal eyes,
not predatory but grieving,
as good animals the body,
not ready, not able to be ready.
La, where did they put
their good body?
This man to my left
will ask me tomorrow
to write home for him,
and I will send the letter
buoyant as a field, characters
dug into yellow-orange firmament,
from the soldiers to all the families,
saying their one lambent thing—

     ∿∿∿∿∿

       You hold my arm so tight,
     dear, that I chafe, I pity you
this first entrance, all faces
       uncurtained. Why

did mother let you come?
Soon you'll start to see
the vestiges of actions,
        nothing startling, just the contours
of attending, of needs, some
                expanding, and some you don't expect,
                        not really frightening—insistent, though.
        And so you must let go
my arm. Everything
                is falling, I mean, evening is falling,
and there are things to do—the little bouquet of bayonets
        in the corner—well, leave them for now.
                        The American flag—well, leave that stuck
                like a hat pin in the topmost tent
                        called night. These men sleep
        in folds of those hems, around tent ropes,
look at how they're tree root and star-flared grass—
        they sleep
                in the shine of our shoes.

Public Woman

Yes, in the hoop cage under my skirt I hide a flask
balanced there for the length of this ride, and when I get out
I'll promenade down the block with no observer the wiser.
Whiskey works to soothe a wound
and loosen a boy up, the same.

Call me nurse—ha!—but I'll keep my crinolines.

I know this terrain, it goes
over the hill, back of the rummaged town, and across the bump
of a man and my untanned leg.

The river is not tame.

I have a red petticoat.

The fan—not necessary—
though lace is essential.
The flask helps.

Mother is amazed at what I get for my *sewing*,
pierce the loop, dot the embroidery, waggle the fringes.

Mother, my handkerchief brings our roast.
Mother, I will cook it.

For the shy ones: I lost my husband to a cannon, let me lean on your shoulder.
For the rugged ones: Now.

They like my bright handkerchief:
ochre hand, carnelian ear, fire hip.

Say scandal and I will say egg.
Hold your nose at me and I will say butter.

My crinolines, the roan horses under my dress.

When I was a girl, my sister and I played Paris
using sticks for easels, smeared cinders
to draw on the backs of envelopes.

Sometimes we'd stand like statues in the Louvre,
dress each other in shawls long as cities,
the Seine always running
indigo and silver
flecked with green.

Out the carriage window, now stopped,
rivers of men turn their heads.
They need medicine.

Sarah Rosetta Wakeman, alias Pvt. Lyons Wakeman

You may wonder why I didn't use my Soldier name
when I got this ring engraved, but use my name from back to home,
Rosetta. I like the way *Rosetta Wakeman* look next to my regiment name,
Co. H 153rd N.Y. Vol., engraved under it,
in those letters that mind me of Castles and moats and such.
And me in and out of the turrets.

I send it to you, Mother, to keep for me.

Someday I'll get out and buy me a farm *in Wisconsin.*
On the Prairie. I'll turn up and hoe that prairie.
This ring will Spark between reins,
these small fingers no one notices. They think it fine
I guard rebs at Carroll Prison.

Right smart building for a prison.
Rebs behind bars want to go home.
Not me, I like to go asoldiering first rate.
I like to go adrilling. *I think a Skirmish drill*
is the prettiest drill that ever was drill.

In the prison they hold three Women. One is a union Major,
she rode her horse and gave orders to the men.

What officer wouldn't ride and give orders
if they is worth a pair of wool Socks?
But they put her in prison.

Marched past the Capitol building they're putting up.
Just a Shell and no top. Like a giant ring.
Too big to use.

〰〰〰〰

Been over a year since I seen a single face I know.
I hear Henry Austin and Cousin Peter Wilder was in town

with the 109 N.Y. regiment over 'cross the river.
I went and found them and *you better believe I had a good visit with them.*

They tell me hay is doing good this year,
hens is laying on and off.

Their faces peel and any minute I think they will say
"Rosetta," just to keep from busting
but they hold in and say Private Lyons to me. So we talked old times
just as if our old times was about the same as ever.

~~~~~

On the Spreading prairie nobody will tell me how to do.
I will Dress as I am a mind to for all anyone else care.

Nobody will get into an *affray* like me and Father.
I am going to raise me some pigs or chickens
and no bother. I will raise what I have a mind to.

I don't believe there are any Rebel's bullets made for me yet.
Nor I don't Care if there is.

~~~~~

I send home a tintype.
How do you like the looks of my likeness,
my face all Serious? Now, don't I march?
I wear full uniform, them winking buttons, cap on Smart,
in my arms that bayonet is good
as a hay rake, and more Shiny.

I am as independent as a hog on the ice.

I want to hear what you think of the tintype.
Father can look at it sometimes.
Do you think I look better than I did
when I was to home?

~~~~~

I never did so good in my life.

I don't hurt much, except once when I moved too fast.

Tell me, *did you peel that hemlock that blowed down in the sugar place?*
What size is that hay barn that you built this summer up on the hill?
Tell me, because I need to know.

We head further south, messes of Swamps and trees with jungle moss.

Mother, can you send me a strong box with a key?

⩘⩘⩘

The likeness you sent of brother looks like him,
but *the artist didn't half finish it off and it rub some and that made it look bad.*

I would like to stand over him with a loaded gun and fixed bayonet
and learn him how to take a likeness.

⩘⩘⩘

Mother, do you still keep the ring?
I like the *Rosetta* engraved nice in it,
cost me 75 cents. I want to see it someday
on my hand that was Soldier.

Did you see the part, Mother, about the iron box?
I need it for my things.

Did the Sugar maples last through the ice storm all right?
Do you remember to feed the Chickens that wander over the south hill?
A little one always gets caught in the ravine
and can't scratch her way back.

⩘⩘⩘

All I ask, Mother, is send me one box,
iron hinges and a key. I want to keep my things Safe
and not Stole by my *good friends.*

I don't hurt much except Nights when I try to sleep.

∿∿∿

I eat but the taste is gone out of it.

The eyes in the swamp is gators.
Some boys use them for target practice.

Just a box, Mother, with iron hinges.

I have enjoyed my self the best
since I have been gone away from home
than I ever did before in my life.

∿∿∿

When I buy my home on the prairie I'll get me some Chickens.
No one can Shoot nor ever be sick again.

Mother, wear the ring for me.

Here all they care about is, shoot them gators.

It will be a home where no one is going to be lonesome for nothing,
rhubarb out the back door, lilac out the side.

On the damn prairie.
I won't allow no bastard to lay down and just not get up.

We'll have Butter three times a day.
You can visit all you want.

Mother Mary Ann Bickerdyke: The Cow Review

My boys have brought me back to the green hillock
on this island in the middle of the Mississippi gulping
around all sides, and they've steadied a field chair.
"Sit," they say, and I won't have all this fuss
like I'm a officer or such, but they insist—
so I let them. Frazier grins hisself silly, hair slicked,
cap stuck on all formal. Charles bellows,
"Bring em on," and here come the cows:
first one's curried to a fine gleam, and now I see
her hoofs is blacked, too, and I swear,
they've tied a canteen around her neck.
Another cow and another, every one of 'em
gleamed and smoothed. Frazier marches along,
shoulders a curry comb like a rifle as he passes.
Clips his mischief eyes to mine.

I found Frazier at night among the row of dead,
clothes froze on him. Held the lantern closer, he exhaled.
Tore my sash off, stanched blood at the belly hole,
hollered for a stretcher. He lived.
Sound as a cow now.

In front of me a Guernsey hulks, lows with curiosity,
the boys prodding her with coffee mugs.
Now come the chickens' plucky staccato
in between cow steps. I remember nettling that rich farmer
to buy us a bovine, and darned if he didn't cough up
a hundred of 'em, then townsfolk followed with a thousand—yep,
a thousand—hens, and we marched 'em all here
to this island to make custard for my boys. Frazier knows.

Charles says, "How do you like your *Cow Review*, Mother?"
And if anybody's unhappy it's no one—not even
them skittery-prissy chickens, on account of here's
some sort of chuckling fuss to be part of. Who'd blame 'em

for wanting that? "Any army," John says,
"can pride themselves on so fine a tattoo as this."
Cows for ambling, chicks for stepping lively.
I remember hearing a while back that General Ulysses
didn't think *me* part of any such fine tattoo.
Still, the old coot loves to rile that colonel
who complains I break rank. As if I give a hoot.
As if I have truck with such stuff as rank. Or file.
"Sorry," Grant says to the colonel, "Can't help you
with Mother Bickerdyke. She outranks me.
She outranks Lincoln!"
                              Gracious, these chickens
outrank us all, so long as they keep
their part of the custard deal. So long as these boys
tote curry combs 'stead of carbines in this trice so long
as the grass is lush. Dear me, enough of lollygag, dillydally,
and dawdle the day—Get me off to the mess hall, haul
me off to camp to start kettles, I've a mess
of taters and six-and-a-half dozen eggs to boil.

But I see the cow in front of me turn a head to Frazier.
Mock serious, face covered with sun, Frazier
stands at attention. Salutes her. How he does go on.

Army of the Cumberland Panel

"Toting belongings hastily packed in knapsacks, slaves flee a Tennessee plantation house on a star-filled winter night to follow the Army of the Cumberland . . . to freedom."

—MARK E. NEELY AND HAROLD HOLZER

The stars have eased their way out of our skins

                               leaving nary a cut.

This silver: varnished stars and our varnished moving
       as we climb out of windows and down lanes,

of our own command.

Oxen and chickens float away.

We walk out of a house into a night.

Nobody home anymore—alone,
      the sky trembles, spills
                exaltation of quiet—

our walking only walking,

following the regiment up the hill—

The Enslaved Mother, Her Baby, and John Brown

I. JOHN BROWN MEETING THEM ON THE STEPS OF THE JAIL

The girl is mine no matter how much you want to put her under the hand
of that man crazy with his hair, his eye like July
        flicking to green-blue behind far-away branches.
                    I know he gave a son
            in that arsenal. Now he walks on
sharpshooter's birdlegs stiff from lying on a stone floor
where the miracle of his belt buckle bent the bayonet's death blow.
                  What makes him tell us God like that,
        like God shakes his clothes in the morning.
              What makes him tell us, You've got to feel blackblood in whiteskin,
                dare whiteskin to eat with you,
makes him clean his revolver at preachers' dinner tables to get a rise out of their wives.
The girl is mine who likes to look at lace, red bandanas, sweetpeas curling.
Clear a way, clear a way.

2. JOHN BROWN'S BLESSING OF THE BABY

Each step takes a breath,
              his leaning, his reaching, his about-to-be placing
        his flint hand on my girl's head,
his eyes a cobalt I turn from,
fear tumbling over in them by the time you look back.

She just wants the white fleece of his face,
              sun-bent fleece to frisk her fingers in.

        Can it be I'm lifting her up to him?
    No, someone—white child maybe in this crowd—is tugging me.

They say John Brown grabbed a whip to punish his son, took him out to the barn,
then made his son use that whip on him,
              each lash for the son's transgressions
                    flaring scarlet down the father's back.

        Don't ask me to use my word on that.
Make a way, make a way.

3. THE LAST MOMENTS OF JOHN BROWN

He descends the stair, stair made of decades
                huddled under it.
Balances mid-step. His hand
                    tests the air in front of him.

There's a noose around his neck
attached to nothing—

beware the loose end.

He and my girl have hooked eyes,
                    but I need my baby's look for me.
            Come away, girl, fold back into mama.

He wept and wept to his wife this morning,
they say, the tears dried a hundred years from now.

He wears his death lightly
on his beard pointing the way,

perdition between each of the gray hairs, and my girl—

                how did we come to raise your elbow like this?
            Whose kiss is this
that in the instant he closes his fire-blue eyes
we might forgive his awed, dry lips on your brow.

He has come, dear, to this stair
just to come to this stair

to look at you

as you pack him in your eye—

Sophronia Bucklin

Not fingers so much as palm. The muscles in it and the face it can make.

My hands could wave through stardust and teach it sparkle,
pick *large black-headed worms* from flesh, extract *fleas from the seams* of uniforms,
and stir puddings too.

I will do this work—made of the strength that comes from holding—
that good labor for which my hands have been so long waiting.

Nights on the cot: I slip on flowers of an unknown color.

Sometimes I watch cows in the field and envy their slow mouthfuls.
Sometimes I watch cavalry horses, proud, wheeling with power, and I grieve their innocence.

〰〰〰

The steward won't allow me to cook eggs for the men on the stove.

So I cook eggs not *on* the stove
but *in* it.

Officers take the good roast for themselves, leave nurses and soldiers
with a dishpan-broth of scraps.
They eat oysters, apple pie.
We, moldy crackers.

The surgeon in charge took my stove away.

I journey to Washington today to buy one with my own money.
I will send it back to the front with me,
I will knead dough for bread and bake it through the night if I have to.

I find *how much the strength of my hands*
        depends *on keeping them steadily employed.*

I will cook whatever I please, for goodness' sake,
when my own stove arrives.

~~~~~

A dog brings baskets of meat to the patients, efficient as any convalescent.
They say the dog was a good soldier at the front:
in the thick of it, kept barking.

If in some moments of some wards,
I could pet a dog under his chin
and he would look straight at me—

and if he would do it with his eyes not borrowed from anything else—

~~~~~

Relieved to be outside, we nurses breathe air slowly,
walk on the field after Gettysburg:

Battered canteens, cartridge-boxes, torn knapsacks, muskets twisted by cannon shot and shell, rusted tin cups,
pieces of rent uniform, caps, belts perforated with shot . . .

Sometimes bodies were so completely wrapped up with the fallen leaves that, unconsciously, I stepped upon them—
the quivering of the loose flesh making my feet unsteady . . .

Still we walk and look for flowers,

and flowers grow pink and amethyst, lacey in the sun,
and we can't help but feel glad to be let out—
green is a friend,
air, refined,

our feet still our feet, and our hands still our hands,
we gather wildflowers and shell fragments.

~~~~~

During the battle, my friend received half a dozen minnie-ball holes in her skirt,
crinoline popping, the steel cage of her hoop skirt dinged with shots
near her ankle and in the cross section by her hip—

Even with *her stay-springs broken,*
not one tear in her flesh.

~~~~~~

Nights on the cot:
>I talk into a stove that roars a song.
>My hands collect blankets of pearls.
>I shake them, the pearls turn red.

Other nights:
>I nurse a puppy who grows into a convalescent
>with a sore paw and broad grin.

Surgeon showed up pickled in the center of the night,
needed the tent pole to prop himself. Drunken scalpel in hand,
he ordered amputations on the spot.

~~~~~~

A man with a small flesh wound in his arm is ordered to have an amputation.
A week later his entire body is bloated and *transparent as glass.*
He dies the next day.

In the amputating room, standing over a patient chloroformed,
surgeon stops a minute, fleam in hand,
to have his picture taken.

~~~~~~

Now surgeon wants to requisition the stove I bought with my own money.

He discharges me. I stand in the kitchen, gingerbread dough on my hands.

Retreat to my tent.
Am reinstated by Dorothea Dix.

Relieved again, then again reinstated,

turned around more times than return can muster.

~~~~~~

Into *my small tent, called the Mortality Tent,* they bring a soldier.

The men come to the tent to give themselves over to fevers, chills,
sometimes to die.

I hand them blankets.

I hear singing in the ward, but can't find the source.
Then find, under bedcovers, contrabands singing their devotions.

When I walk back to the Mortality Tent, hymns thrum at my neck,
when I stir pudding, hymns bubble to the surface.

I remember how strong my hands were . . .

If they could iron the field,
shake it, spank it away

my hands might ring, shout, croon, lisp,

might never lose grip of this spoon.

3 NAMES FROM THE WHEEL

Union Camp Music

After the rebs across the river play their "Swanee" song,

we sit with silence cramping our knees and shoulders. Until Lewis stands with his cornet—then we all stand, and our whole band plays at the rebs, trumpets and saxhorns a goin'.

Some play over the shoulder brass horns, turn backs to the river to blow music behind them—and damn if we don't aim "Battle Hymn of the Republic" right at their faces.

But the rebs are up for it, they answer with a polka. A bit bothersome coming from the other side—

that it can sound so sweet.

Evening orange, fringed in the trees,
riverwater sliding notes across,

and our boys play something from a opera, with a fife to go more lively. When the song sprouts into that slow sky I do believe they holler us up on the other shore—

then come on with a Irish jig and of course Lewis can't help but pick a harmony on his cornet and Joshy plays too, poppin' drumsticks to right the beat.

And I see my wife and baby in the orange-lit music. Strange, that I can do a good thing just listening.

〰〰〰

Any other evening our boys only play for the owls and us, outcricket the crickets, going late to keep us warm. Mules bray along.

Lewis got drunk once, fell and flattened that cornet almost to a fan, tassels spread in the mud and freezing up. When he's sober he plays like the wind. Then the wind gets real jealous and notches it up a gear.

Colonel paid Lewis a good price to join up. On account of his talent.

Joshy says he's fifteen, but he's twelve sure as he ever ate one spoonful of raspberry jam from home. Nights, he sets down his drum, small circle inside the wagon wheel, curls up around it.

〰〰〰

And all I know how to do is balance a horse with a plow and remember Mary and our baby, the three of us going to church Sunday mornings.

My Uncle Lorne can balance a fiddle with a bow, saw jigs to fall huskings, where a while back he got me to cider, and then to dancing with Mary.

And I don't know why there's a thing the music does.

And I never thought the secesh could do it to us.

~~~~

One time we skirmished, Ned holding a sword in one hand, a bugle in the other. Hector stuck a fife in his belt and ran ready with a bottle of spirits to help our boys.

I'm telling you, nobody can hear that fife, that drum, without they want to march along, leave their home, want to not hear their wife calling them to dinner.

Then they play the next song, and it makes you want to hear nothing but your wife calling you to dinner.

~~~~

We holler across the shore for the rebs to cease fire—their music-fire, you know.

But they won't have it, keep tootling parts of jigs, and our boys keep tootling other parts till they land on "Lorena" and they do it together, and loud—from both sides of the river, louder now, banjo, harmonica,

and Lewis looks like he never done nothin' else, and Joshy looks like he's home for each strike of the snare,

and we're in the middle of our own voices gone honeyed and howling,

and I'm singin', damn it, sure as singers pull air,

and it may be that Mary brushes her hair at home, hand tracking the gleam,

and it may be that this blast of mouths, this flaring of bells
sure as *the sun can never dip so low*, as our faces turn

the orange of clouds, a pitch that shapes and holds us

I'm here to tell you, that this singing,

that this damned singing troubles,

that this singing troubles

nothing.

Making Havelocks for the Volunteers

Heads bent, we pull sharp steel
                        through the weave of havelocks,
       official military headgear with curtains
made for necks vulnerable to desert sun.
It doesn't matter that we have no desert.

Baskets of them, done, appendaged with visors and slack flaps.

We don't need to look out the windows but only
                  at threads and planes of light,
swaths of material over our knees, skirts buoyed.

A philodendron spreads wild in one corner, and in the other
            the American flag drapes dim stripes on the wall.

Cousins, we could be, with our same devout styles,
hair pulled to the nape, knowing mouths, brows
            fatigued by the task
                  and perhaps by our ruffles.

When fingers riddle cloth no one looks up from her compassing work
         except for a moment when
finished, in the second after knotting a thread,

I slap a newly needled havelock on my head

just to feel the brisk of it for a moment
             before it's consigned to the basket.

Monticello, Early 1865

"The place was once very pretty, but it has gone to ruin now . . . the ball room [dome room] is on the second floor, and has a thousand names scratched over its walls . . ."

The roses have gone to leaves,
the gnarled cabernets dried to the roots.

Still, Mr. Jefferson would be pleased we continue at his university
set at the bottom of the hill where lawless, the land crumples,
a bill you could stuff in your wallet.

Blood fights blood, still we persevere at our studies.

But this morning Jimmy and I climb up to see
Mr. Jefferson's shattered panes and sodden eaves,
walk first through the meadow, touching half-wild cows
on the tops of their heads, their curious ears turning with disapproval.
The estate bunches, asleep, as an arm after a long night resting
under a head, waking to nerves tossed like grain, tossed on fire—

Watch for the broken steps, Jimmy—

And we're in the house now, headed past the parlor
where Mr. Jefferson pulled a bow across the vines of his violin
urging guests to dance on the parquet floor, not knowing
one day his attic would grow to bats,
flour to mice, outbuildings to feral pigs.
He'd be as appalled at the vermin as he was at the miracles

he ripped out of his Bible—not just miracles out of *one* Bible,
but four different ones, in four different languages.
He didn't believe in them—divine interventions, the reason-defying kind—
so he tore the offending pages, did it fourfold.
That's a lot of miracles.

And what's left of the man, the country, now that we live in a town given up
to the likes of Custer, mustard-haired ruffian
who stayed mounted while my professor ran

back to his house and ripped the sheet off his bed to make a flag
and wave Mr. Jefferson's university to surrender?
Curse Custer—the bastard spared us our buildings but took our beards.

Jimmy and I step now toward the dome room
that rounds over the parlor, the place Mr. Jefferson called his "sky room,"
become in our fancy a century-long sky.

We walk the hallway, dark, to a thin staircase.

Silas and Henry were here last year for the joust,
horse hooves splitting the lawn. Soldiers from the hospital,
some with only one arm, held reins in their mouths,
aimed jousting rods at rings, and shared apples
with the town girls glancing around as they sat on blankets
snapped from sequestered family trunks. Today,

Jimmy and I want something different,
want to go beyond the lawn, the hall, up this blocked staircase
to mount the sky room,

want to reach the dome with round windows circling like planets
where Mr. Jefferson in the old days would have watched
the whole farm from every direction,

want to glance the floor that stays the precise grass green
Gilbert Stuart mixed from one of his paintings
and scraped onto paper so Mr. Jefferson could take it home,

to shoulder the door wedged by bloat, to put our weight to it and lurch

sudden inside those curved walls
that shimmer with the thousand names

      of interlopers, Union and Confederate who camped at Monticello
          over nights and weeks, came to find the clemency of secret,
              like what Jeff Davis gave us in finishing our law studies,
          our diplomas rifling the day before we go to the field of war—

                and it may happen any time,

and it may be—it certainly is—
         that the law has no jurisdiction over such waste,
  the law as it files its grasses—

and we want to walk this minute into that sky room

and read the myriad names of soldiers who scratched signatures in every direction,
shingled the place to the inch with angled hands,

want to finger the marks,
add ours to the criss-cross,

Jimmy lying down, digging his in a space just above the floor
and I etching mine with the "i" dotted by a script already there,

crimped between one man's last name and another man's first,

the line of my person at once jutted and recovered,
to write in one motion.

Phantom Limb

Lowell, one of my favorite men, sits propped in bed, white face, white neck against the white tent wall.

The ice this morning over all the tents. Camp one great single-ice-sheet, turrets simple and glowing.

Lowell talks as if we're brother and sister, I feel warm for moments.

I think of saviors as those the wind sticks to—flying hair crests and levels about them.

No saviors here, but I remember them in my picture books to home from when I was little.

Yes, I wring my fingers, for the warmth.

Lowell had his right arm amputated.
Then his left.

At twilight the deer come to us. Of course their eyes are not compassionate but you do think such things in the reflection off the mauve snow.

At night I hear the *Lost Battalion* stepping soft as twilit deer carefully around our tents.

The men of the *Lost Battalion* speak fourteen languages. They don't know how to give orders to each other. But they stay here to guard us.

When he first saw his right arm on the floor Lowell thought, Good, *There is the pain, and here am I.*

I get used to it, amaze myself with my cast heart.

Poor Lowell told me one arm will itch and he'll try to scratch it with the other arm.

If I was missing a hand, an arm, another hand, well—

Once I forgot to put my apron on and couldn't remember if my body was hanging on the hook.

I talk nonsense sometimes, but of course I know I'm doing it.

Eight steps lead to this flap.
Two cardinals trim the elms.

The *Lost Battalion* will never find their commander, I don't think they know which side they're on.

They'll guard us as long as we need them, which is for eras. They mix up their cuffs with their collars.

They can say *hello* and *sleep well* interchangeably.
They say, *Gut*, when they walk stumblingly and *Dieu!*, when at ease.

A new shipment of jams coming in. Up at the Armory once we had ice cream.

To think of good things. My aunt Nettie's sewing box covered with coral-pink flowers. Mama's bracelet she'd let me spin on her arm when I was little.

Actually, the wind. My face in it.

Right outside the flaps there, the wind curves around a corner. A horse rushes to overtake something.

The smell of decay intense as vinegar. Blood that runs unembarrassed.

Forget the hole in the abdomen you could put your hand through to the other side. Forget the glossy, glossy skin on the stump.

And does the phantom limb yearn for its body?

Forget the man from Andersonville who cannot remember his name, who walks and stares—he came to us, his face green, mold growing on it.

And do I yearn for—what?

Another prisoner says he wants to go back to the front to fight, that *the rebels had boarded him eight months,* and he's anxious to go back and *settle his bill of fare!*

You start to breathe the cough.

You start to look at your own arms strangely.

Though ghosts, the deer don't blame anyone for it.
They get their bodies back during the day.

The wind might blow away their ears, might blow off every single cap of a color.
It might leave the men their skin.

I need to check the cardinals today to see if they remember how to dress in wings.

May it please the wind not to take them.

Next week Lowell will go to the Stump Hospital, that's what they call it.

He knows. He reaches for me to ask for water. Reaches with his eyes.

I see his cupping fingers.

Gettysburg Cyclorama, Southwest Panel

"The cyclorama is a mammoth oil painting, fifty feet high and four hundred feet long, stretched around the wall of the building and viewed by the spectator from its center, the effect being that of looking over the surrounding country from a slight elevation . . . Emerging from a winding staircase on to the central platform, the visitor seems suddenly transported from Boston to the battle-field of Gettysburg . . . The view is apparently prolonged to the horizon . . ."

—*THE BUDGET*, DECEMBER 21, 1884

"It is difficult, and in some places impossible, to tell where the canvas leaves off and the artificial foreground begins."

—THE *SUNDAY HERALD*, DEC. 21, 1884

". . . in one instance, it is quite impossible to distinguish a painted cannon from an actual one which lies near it."

—THE *DAILY TRANSCRIPT*, DEC. 30, 1884

We hold each other so we know where we're going.
Me, Robert Bird, with bandaged arm and my brother, Peter, thigh wrapped.
With one hand he leans on me, with the other holds a crutch that is actually a sword.
Smoke wraps us. Blood doesn't run under these tons of paint,
it thumbs us under its weight,
but that's better than some panels lost in attics moldy with blue.
Other panels the Shoshone cut up to sew tents—
as they're beading capes and scraping elk hides,
they can see a battle again every day.
Union horses ride behind their sleep.

Peter and me, lucky to be alive, were mustered the same day,
but we're in a battle we never fought, and none of the rest of our company are here.
In back of us everyone still fights, even though we're already bandaged.
Pickett's on a horse he didn't ride in a charge I didn't see.
We shuffle past the dead horse, past wagon wheels.
We look and the attack is a circle
and we go round again.

      On a platform in the middle a girl stands
to view us, her lips slack, eyes intent. Not
to cry. To take it in and still
be herself, which of course she can't.

To the side of her, two veterans weep,
a mother tends the railing for balance.
Emerging from the oil color, in front,
a blasted tree, clods of earth, part of a broken fence.

Peter and I know these people can't walk in without bleeding,
they see paint sway in the panels, a million cries flying.

The people on the platform work hard not to betray us.

No matter where you look the eye
cannot but be filled with this.

Peter Bird

August 12, 1862. Robert and me enlisted together mustered next day to Gettysburg.

November 7, 1862. *Very cold weather with much suffering no rations issued except Sugar. Troops subsisting on parched corn which they gather from the fields.*

It will be years before I wed Mary & we move upstate Michigan to the lighthouse on Keweenaw peninsula. I'll be first keeper.

November 9, 1862. *General McCleland & Burnside at Head Quarters many of the boys go to see them. Say they frequently refreshed themselves with potations from the same canteen.*

Above our tents I see sparrows sleep in tree limbs beaks stuck in their feather tents.

June 12, 1863. *Marched from Camp Way 5 ½ am halted at Harwood to execute prisoner wood for desertion . . .*

I've seen a sparrow separated by a cannon ball.
Feathers fall in petals.

I'm hit. Lay on a rutted field my leg to be taken four days I lay, hold my leg to keep it. Wish for more pain, a little more, to keep me there.

Years later at Keweenaw a sparrow riffles past my daughter, ridged wings, late sun.

In a feed store I can tell by the boys' faces I won't come through, thigh shattered. Pine floor smells like woods.

I will die I will walk with a limp, die, I will pull my hip behind me,

die, I will keep the light at eagle harbor, 1876 in the Keweenaw, Mary Jane & the children. Water makes a body around us.

The lighthouse holds sun up lights the spray.
I'm first keeper, I keep
the light, seagulls, ghosts, sky.

The storms don't come often.
The nights daily.

Gettysburg Cyclorama, Northwest Panel

"A real stone fence is continued by a painted one . . ."
—BOSTON DAILY ADVERTISER, DEC. 23, 1884

The viewers miss shadows of clouds breathing across the land.
Not able to quell first impressions of the trinkets in front:
how the built part of a wooden wagon melts into a painted wagon,
or a placed portion of charred tree recedes to a painted tree,
one leg of tripod over a well, actual,
and the other two legs brushed on. I could hand you my
hat and it would drop into color
in your hand, but you have to know
that I swing cumulus over your shoulder
to the beat of blood in your ears. You hear it.
They heard it, 1863, clouds that were patient thrushes.
And standing under this tree, 1883,
in the deepest shade of the panels, I, Philippoteaux,
painter of this cyclorama, lean on a tree trunk,
my sword drawn but bowed to the ground
for as long as anyone can glimpse it.
The photographer shot the landscape photographs
showing me as the only man on the field, and now I remain
the only man standing in this brushed field where I've oiled myself in,
eyes scraping across the fall and swell and running
and cringing and pocking of men. The lunging. One man,
a freed slave, carries a stretcher. The front end of it
will be ripped away altogether for a later artist
in 1913 to dot in two blue buckets to haul instead.
But the clouds keep growing into rocks into thrushes.
I can rub sienna into the rim-rutted road, can slip
magenta into the banner's mad slapping,
can do it with the finesse of a child
who controls his breathing perfectly
as he pretends to sleep, I shape
clouds carrying umber
to the tree I stand
under, ready,
here, to dry.

Cornelia Hancock

For the Gettysburg wounded, wagons of provisions arrive. I pull bread into pieces, find a stick to spread jelly, pass it to hundreds on a shingle-board tray.

I walk among men who cry out.

It took nearly five days for some three hundred surgeons to perform the amputations.

Dr. Frederick Dudley says he would rather lose ten other nurses and keep me in his hospital.

Do not worry about me. I never get sick and *am safer here than in the attic at home, where I do get scared.*

〜〜〜

We had *a splendid dinner—Ham, Eggs, Oyster pie, Roast Beef and potatoes, peach tarts and cup custards . . . Dr. Dudley said he enjoyed having them which he is seldom known to say.*

I received thy letter. Please send more bandages. We have all we want of meat but nothing of bandages.

Dudley will get me a heating stove for my quarters.

Do not ask me about politics. I care nothing for it.

A private's eyes are open, and sight being what it is, it must place itself on something, and finds a shelf in me. His eyes do not register, do not look either in or out, but only restate my face—

I tell you I have lost my memory almost entirely but it is gradually returning.

〜〜〜

The hospital cars trudge off with amputated limbs, their *groaning load—and think I to myself, the idea of making a business of maiming men is not one worthy of a civilized nation.*

〜〜〜

Dr. Dudley has lost some of the reserve around the eyes, though he keeps it around his mouth.

After rounds, he talks of the beauties of the body, not blushing—then remembers it is to me he speaks.

〜〜〜

We have started marching—no one will tell us where.

Dudley has been captured on the field. Loyal, he stayed with his soldiers. Their location not certain.

I am thinner than I was. I will probably return to you *ninety-years old*.

I see everyone around me has turned ninety-years old.

Dudley, somewhere in the narrow unknown.

I wash a boy's head after days of marching and find a face around his eyes.

〰〰〰

We have marched, and we will march.

I send you *the Black thread, . . . the length of half the bosom of my corset, the white thread half the waist.* I would like two corsets made, please.

Still no destination. We march till the *skin is off my toes.*

Please send thy daughter a tablecloth or ribbon or something pretty.

I do not mind if we march as far as Richmond. And past that,

and past that.

Woman at the Fence

I was out looking for it—

that was before all my hens died,
someone poisoned them—

was out looking for the *dead line.*

Looked in the thickets, the muck, and the woods
but I can't find it, where the thing turns,

where there's a fringe of long sounds
from the wisps that might be groans, curses,
palpate palpate palpate shut
the door to that man's ear.

I cannot tell any more about the dooryard of love.

That was before my clouds died,
just closed up one by one into flat white cambric
                                    and swallowed themselves.
I wonder if someone poisoned the clouds, too.

You look at me as if my eyes were red,
                    my eyes aren't red, I see fine,

I don't pick at myself except when I have to.

I don't know a single person here.

Every morning my hair falls out in the brush,
I feel very pretty,
but that was thirty mirrors ago.

My children, all of them poisoned,
but that may be my cats—

They say on the field the moon will snap

                              the small rocks into smoke.

Once I found a man still alive next to a fence,
a boy, blond, his hair, dotted
with white
            where he'd been knocked on the head.

I rocked his shoulder to sleep
and inside, the pain
widened to white.
I let him go.

Tell you what,
if you ever find that line
just don't tell me.

I wash my son's shirt and the sleeves fall off in the water.

4 A PIN-STAR STARTS

Unnamed Panels

Panel in cobalt

If I'm lying on this slope,
head facing down the low
roll, a question:
if I've been hurt.

Grackle sidesteps a limb, spider
lumbers across a hand, grass
whirrs. The eye never stops moving
toward what is moving.

Note: downhill
from me, a body
stills, but could
jig with trees,

finish irrelevant.
Something to the side of me
thrashes. The wind tunes
branches. Hum to keep

from rising too far,
a two-second aria.
I can't twist over
or reach this arm

to the strap, thirst to fill,
cloud to brim,
between stretched
oak limbs—

Note: the grackle looks
staples into me.
I turn my head to
a rock, not rock

but a dent under it,
rest my supplication
at the twig-claws
birds use to mark air—

Panel of Golds

Once in a while my ring,
cold, becomes colder,
a kind of comfort
for the length of a while

when sight turns
limber as branches'
hymn hymn hymn
spreading.

Light jogs this branch.
Sun all afternoon, volume,
flowers flaming
from the dirt.

A sulfur thread, the soonest
war monument, trees try
to handle it themselves with green
openings, slappings,

manage it with a whiff
of ash to idle through clouds.
My ring is here.
I can't see my finger

RED CURVING PANEL

We're arranged on this hill
where bats spill upwards
as ripped snoods
and dart contours

around knee, hip, shoulder—crisp
as they are careful,
and I lie with bitter weeds,
longing—for what—

And all the blood sent to that—
My shoulder—I don't
know which side,
back shellacs to front,

and a heart in the turn—
beats the same as the flapping
ditties that yield to me
warm and holy bats—

Iridescent panel with green crenellations

The ant doesn't
detour this clump, goes
right over, muscularity,
waterbag blood

of it, shiny lobes,
six hooves
of it, chomping—
I could list

to this task,
tie a look
to the dogged
scrambling, but

a pin-star starts
to push the sun aside—
and how to count
that rhythm?

I suppose you could say
fireflies—dab
—dab—flame-
whip across

a spangled grass.
But ant,
gone now,
but fireflies,

doused.
But
I am
afraid

Song panel

A person's face shapes
to singing, turns
waves placid, easing
to other waves, more placid.

Cold is a colder.
Oh hard times come again
no more: Let me keep them
outside *my cabin door*—

A person's face sings
and the back of her neck does
too, strong neck muscles better
than omens, and a fine hair blows

across her mouth, following
the *frail forms fainting*
at the door. She sings
not for anything in particular

except for what the voice metes
out, not to reach her hand at *more*.
I see in calico, see in grains
the rosin on the bow,

see through it to notes'
intervals, *hard times*
come again no more. Snow—
is it snowing? Squirrels know

to feel sun in white-weight,
colder than solace,
snow as a steadfast.
The deer are lifting

Blank

At first she'll think she has
no right to the grief
my body harnesses,
that she can't presume

for me and she'll shift,
floating chaff, as she sleeps
in what's left of the remaining,
portion the proven

as melody. I wouldn't say
life drains. I'd say
non-life, a mill,
gathers in the blades.

A shred hangs
from a grackle's mouth,
each year for decades their beaks
will remember gathering—

PANEL OF DASHES AND CROSSHATCHES

For year-stretched hours hunger

tolls, then hardens

to seed, compresses bone, lapses

vein to furrow, snow won't land.

Ants know to stay in,

grackles don't matter,

palms indigo.

In tatters, cloth strips among gray

grasses, a button presses

on my wrist and skin turns

wood-smooth as a plow handle.

Singers wave one lip now. Wind

throws itself in all directions

through tassled corn, beautiful, heaved,

the faint maize smell

breathes me

Notes

The poems in this collection were inspired by many sources: paintings, memoirs, panels from a cyclorama, panel from a panorama, letters, engravings, diaries, songs, illustrations, and photography. Direct quotations have been italicized. Sources include the following:

"Sarah Emma Edmonds": memoir from 1861–1865, *Soldier, Nurse, Spy*, 1865.

"Susie King Taylor": memoir from 1862–1865, *Reminiscences of My Life in Camp*, 1902.

"Off for the War / Home from the War": Currier and Ives, three images published in the same year, 1861. The first two, *Off for the War: The Soldier's Adieu* and *Home from the War: The Soldier's Return*, depict a foot soldier's family with a modest house and clothing. The third, the Special Officers' Edition of *Home from the War: The Soldier's Return*, offers a retouched version of the second drawing in which the foot soldier is now an officer with a horse and the woman and boy wear fine clothes, the three of them grouped in more opulent surroundings.

"The War Spirit at Home": Lilly Martin Spencer, oil on canvas, 1866. The commentary on the painting is from Mark E. Neely and Harold Holzer, *The Union Image: Popular Prints of the Civil War North*, 2000.

"Process of Drafting in New York": illustration, "Process of drafting in the 6th District in New York, August 19," *Harper's Weekly*, 1863.

"Colonel Ely S. Parker": photograph by Mathew Brady, *Grant and His Staff during the Final Campaign*, 1864. (Material is also included from William Armstrong's *Warrior in Two Camps* and Raymond J. Herek's *These Men Have Seen Hard Service*.)

"Women's Sanitary Corps": painting by Anna Mays, 1861–1865.

"Sarah Rosetta Wakeman": letters from 1862–1864, written by Sarah Rosetta Wakeman, alias Pvt. Lyons Wakeman, collected in *An Uncommon Soldier*, edited by Lauren Cook Burgess.

"Mother Mary Ann Bickerdyke: The Cow Review": some information about Mary Ann Bickerdyke is from *The Part Taken by Women in American History*, Mrs. John A. Logan, 1912. (Given the mention of Ulysses S. Grant in the poem, I want to add that of all Grant quotations, my favorite is this: "There never was a time when, in my opinion, some way could not be found to prevent the drawing of the sword.")

"Army of the Cumberland, a Panel": from a panorama, by William Delaney Travis, 1864–1865.

"The Enslaved Mother, Her Baby, and John Brown": three different paintings, including *John Brown Meeting the Slave Mother and Her Child on the Steps of Charleston [sic] Jail on His Way to Execution . . .* , by Currier and Ives, after Louis L. Ransom, 1863; *John Brown's Blessing*, by Thomas Satterwhite Noble, 1867; *The Last Moments of John Brown*, by Thomas Hovenden, 1884.

"Sophronia Bucklin": memoir from 1862–1865, *In Hospital and Camp*, 1869.

"Union Camp": several tales of such wartime musical exchanges exist. Lyric from the widely popular song of the period, "Lorena," written by H. D. Webster and J. P. Webster, 1857.

"Making Havelocks for the Volunteers": wood engraving by Winslow Homer, *The War—Making Havelocks for the Volunteers*, 1861.

"Monticello, Early 1865": Epigraph quoted from Monticello.org website. The story of the thousand names was probably apocryphal. Other information was gleaned from Melvin Urofsky's *The Levy Family and Monticello, 1834–1923*, Marc Leepson's *Saving Monticello*, and Jack Mclaughlin's *Jefferson and Monticello: Biography of a Builder*.

"Phantom Limb": "The Case of George Dedlow," attributed to S. Weir Mitchell, *Atlantic Monthly*, 1866. (Sophronia Bucklin mentions the "Lost Battalion" that speaks fourteen languages; Anna Morris Holstein's *Three Years in Field Hospitals of the Army of the Potomac*, 1867, mentions the soldier who wants to go back to the front because he has a "bill of fare" to settle.)

"Cyclorama of the Battle of Gettysburg, Southwest Panel": a cyclorama painting by Paul Philippoteaux, 1883. Newspaper quotations about the 1884 showing of the *Cyclorama* in Boston are cited in Dean S. Thomas's *The Gettysburg Cyclorama*.

"The Diary of Peter Bird": by Peter Bird, 24th Michigan Infantry, 1862, Wayne Historical Museum, Michigan.

"Cyclorama of the Battle of Gettysburg, Northwest Panel": by Paul Philippoteaux, 1883.

"Cornelia Hancock": Hancock's letters, 1863–1864, collected in *Letters of a Civil War Nurse*, edited by Henrietta Stratton Jacquette, 1998.

"Song Panel," section in "Unnamed Panels": lyrics from "Hard Times Come Again No More," by Stephen Foster, 1854.

POETS OUT LOUD *Prize Winners*

Daneen Wardrop

Cyclorama

Terrence Chiusano

On Generation & Corruption

EDITOR'S PRIZE

Sara Michas-Martin

Gray Matter

Peter Streckfus

Errings

EDITOR'S PRIZE

Amy Sara Carroll

Fannie + Freddie: The Sentimentality of Post–9/11 Pornography

Nicolas Hundley

The Revolver in the Hive

EDITOR'S PRIZE

Julie Choffel

The Hello Delay

Michelle Naka Pierce

Continuous Frieze Bordering Red

EDITOR'S PRIZE

Leslie C. Chang
Things That No Longer Delight Me

Amy Catanzano
Multiversal

Darcie Dennigan
Corinna A-Maying the Apocalypse

Karin Gottshall
Crocus

Jean Gallagher
This Minute

Lee Robinson
Hearsay

Janet Kaplan
The Glazier's Country

Robert Thomas
Door to Door

Julie Sheehan
Thaw

Jennifer Clarvoe
Invisible Tender